Pat Grillo

Intro to Line Dancing

Self Published 2023

Sponsored by:

©01-13-2023 by Pat Grillo. All rights reserved
Photocopying prohlibited with out permission of the author.

If you don't know the steps,
how can you line dance?

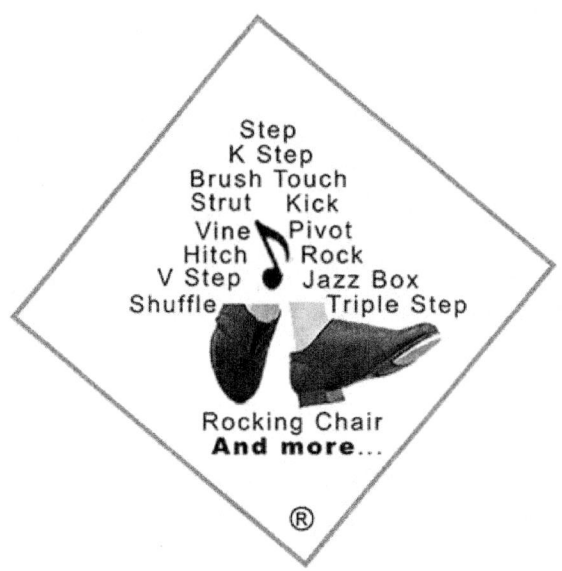

It's going to be fun !

Table of Contents

Intro
Why I Dance 5
Benefits
Physical 6
Mental 7
Floor Layout
Layout 8
Tips 9
Dance Structure 10
Find the Beat 11
Lets Dance
Steps & Touches 12
Intro to Dance List 13
Step Touch Dances 14-30
Syncopated Dances 31-41
List of Steps Learned 42
How to Read a Step Sheet .. 43
How-to Glossary 46
Notes 49
Links 51

IV

Why You Should Line Dance

"Enjoy yourself while exercising your body and mind"

In order to experience the full benefits of line dancing, you must be willing to learn. You need to take time to familiarize yourself with the dance floor, understand the dance structure and recognize the names of the basic steps.

I was 69 years old when I discovered the joy of line dancing. After 3 years of dancing, I begin teaching and leading groups. Today, at age 77, I am an accomplished dancer and instructor.

Over the years, line dancing has improved my physical health and mental attitude. It has also given me the gift of self-satisfaction.

Come dance with me, it's going to be fun.

"Add years to your life and life to your years."

Improve Physical Health

Benefits

Control Balance
Develop Coordination
Improve Flexibility
Control Cholesterol

Increase Stamina
Burn Calories
Improve Posture
Strengthen Muscles

Dance your way to a healthy body

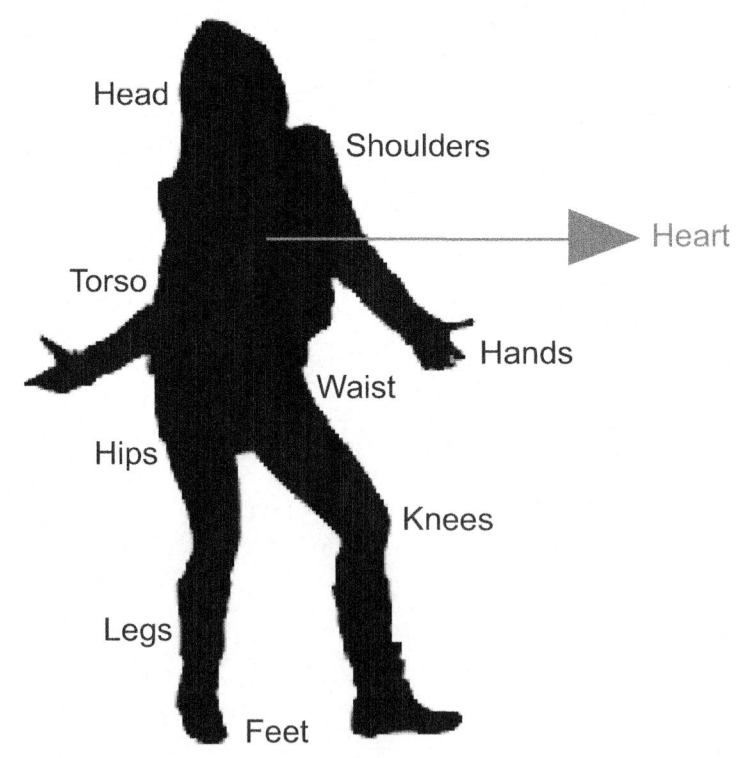

Build Mental Strength

Benefits

Build Confidence	Ease Anxiety
Combate Dementia	Relieve Stress
Control Hypertension	Elevate Mood
Control Hyperactivity	Enhance Memory
Control Depression	Enrich Self-esteem
Develop Purpose	Increase Concentration

Relax and soothe your mind with music

Floor Layout

There are no set directional rules in line dancing. The direction you turn or the number of walls you move to is the choreographer's discretion. So, if you are not familiar with the steps to a particular dance, you need to train yourself to listen closely to the leader's instructions.

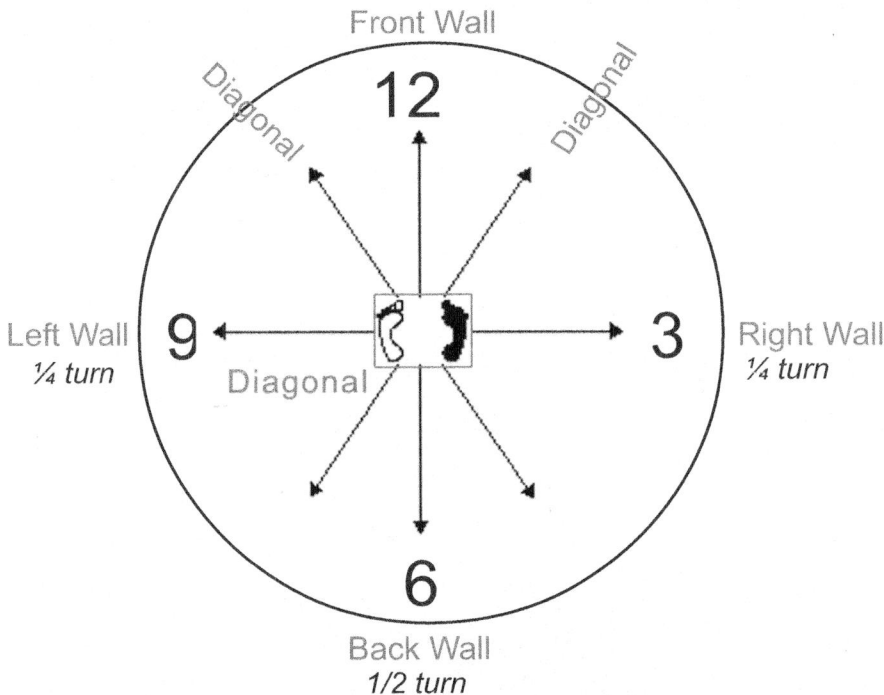

Tips to Ponder

1. **Take small steps:** helps keep you in sync with the music
2. **Keep Moving:** never stop moving. If you find yourself off-beat or have forgotten the next step, fake it until you find a familiar place to continue the routine

Tips

1. Wear sensible shoes; no flip-flops. You will find dancing much more safe wearing closed in footwear.
2. Start each dance with feet together and weight on the correct foot.
3. Keep knees flexible; no bending or locking.
4. Tuck hips in a bit; don't stick your rear out.
5. Keep your back and shoulders relaxed and straight.
6. Hold your head up straight; important for both balance and control.
7. Don't look at your own feet or someone else's while dancing. When your head is down, your balance can be thrown off or if the person makes a mistake, so will you. Memorizing the steps will build self-confidence.
8. Be aware of step length. The correct step length is shoulder width. If you take large steps outside your body frame, you may lose your balance or coordination as well as knock yourself off beat.

Dancing in front of a mirror or recording a video of yourself dancing will increase your self-awareness.

Dance Structure

Beginner dances generally consist of 32 steps. The steps are broken down into four sections of eight and are referred to as a sequence. The 32 step sequence repeats itself throughout the routine.

Sequence

1-8 Section 1
1-8 Secton 2
1-8 Section 3
1-8 Section 4

} 32 Steps

Routine

A routine starts on the first beat following the introduction and ends on the last beat of the music.

Walls

All dances start on the front wall (12 o'clock). Dances are choreographed to dance on one, two, or four walls. Located at the top of the step sheet, you will find the number of walls a dance entails. For more step sheet information, go to page 44.

One-wall Dance

The entire routine starts and ends on the front wall.

Two-wall Dance

The dance routine is performed on the front and back walls. Each 32 step sequence ends and restarts on the front or back wall.

Four-wall Dance

The dance is performed on all 4 walls and will repeat itself on all 4 walls throughout the dance routine. When dancing a 4-wall dance expect to sometimes make a full-turn, quarter-turn half-turn, or a three-quarter turn in the sequence. Follow your step sheets carefully and listen to the leader.

Find the Beat

The beat is generally the loudness sound you hear in the music and is referred to as the *snare drum.* it sounds like a hand clap or a snapping of the fingers. Other instruments will be playing, but you need to always focus on the loudest sound because it is the beat. The beat is organized in an 8 count series which repeats itself throughout the music.

A song length is generally 2:45 to 3:25 minutes long. The dancer will begin dancing on the snare (first beat following the introduction). Each step syncs with each beat in the music.

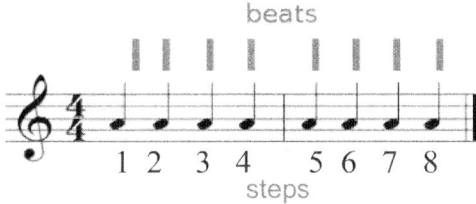

How to Find the Beat

Think of music like you would a paragraph. Both start with an introduction and then moves on to the story or *lyrics* This is when and where you will find the beat. It can be tricky!

Follow the Leader

If you are not familiar with the music, it can be very difficult to find the beat. Since introductions are many and varied from song to song, it is important to listen and follow the leader's directions.

Count the Beats

No matter who you are, what your musical background is, or how skilled you are at feeling the music, counting always elevates your dance. The purpose of counting is to give structure to the dance steps so that the eight step count will match perfectly with the eight beats.

Steps & Touches
Let us begin at the beginning

It is essential you learn and understand the difference between a step and a touch before you begin dancing. A step is when you switch your weight from one foot to the other. A touch is when you *do not change weight.* Every step or touch must sync with a beat in the music.

Step: 1 count
Shift and move weight from one foot to the other

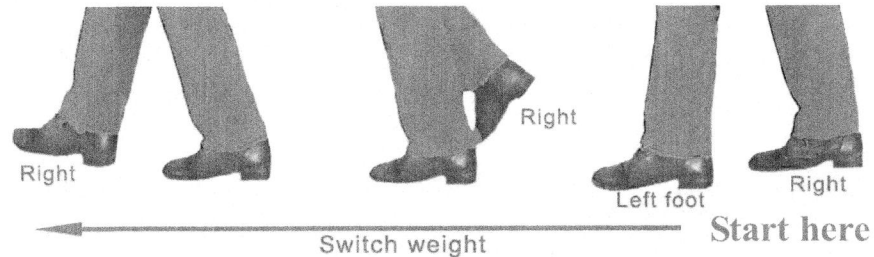

Touch: 1 count
Do not switch weight; use the same foot for the next step

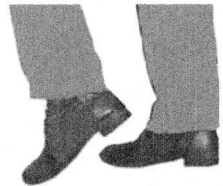

Other 1-count Steps

Bump	Heel-touch	Skate
Brush	Hitch	Slide
Cross	Hold	Stomp
Flick	Rock	Tap
Kick	Scuff	Toe-touch

Step Sheet List

Now that you are familiar with the dance floor, it's time to turn on the music and get started learning the steps. The following pages consist of step sheets which will progressively introduce you to the basic steps as well as familiarize you with reading a step sheet. The more you dance the more confidence you will gain and the more fun you will have.

Step Sheets

Steps & Touches 14	Two Step 32
Cupid Shuffle 15	EZ Shuffle 33
Rainy Night 16	Honey I'm Good 34
Electric Slide 17	Live Laugh Line Dance . 35
Eye Candy EZ 18	River Bank 36
I Fall in Love EZ 19	Monkey Around 37
Blackpool by the Sea.... 20	Jack I'm Mellow 38
Funky Town EZ............. 21	Broke and Beautiful 39
Ten Tonne Truck EZ 22	Chilly Cha Cha 40
Cowboy For a Night...... 23	High Class 41
Be Bop EZ 24	
Livin' on Love EZ 25	
Sure You Are 26	
Chocolate Melon 27	
Country Line 28	
Come Dance With Me .. 29	

Step and Touch

Count: 32 **Wall:** 2 **Level:** Absolute Beginner
Choreographer: Pat Grillo - 2022
Music: High Low and In Between, Mark Wills
Honky Tonk Habits, Emillo Navair

Start: Vocals -- Weight on left foot (counter clockwise

Section 1: Step, Together, Step, Touch (R&L)

- 1-2   Step R foot 1/8 diagonal fwd, step L next to R
- 3-4   Step R foot fwd, touch L next to right
- 5-6   Step L foot 1/8 fwd, step R next to L
- 7-8   Step L foot fwd, touch R next to L

Section 2: Backward Step and Heel Touch 4X

- 1-2   Step R foot backward, touch L heel in place
- 3-4   Step L foot backward, touch R heel in place
- 5-6   Step right backward, touch L heel in place
- 7-8   Step left backward, touch R heel in place

Section 3: K Step

- 1-2   Step R foot 1/8 diagonally fwd, touch L foot next to right foot
- 3-4   Step L foot back to center, touch R foot next to left foot
- 5-6   Step R foot 1:8 diagonally back, touch L foot next to left foot
- 7-8   Step L foot to center, touch R foot next to left

Section 4: Walk Around

- 1-2   Step R to right side, touch left foot next to R (RL)
- 3-4   Turn L ¼ left (weight to left foot), touch R next to L (wall 9)
- 5-6   Step R to right side, touch L foot next to R (RL)
- 7-8   Turn ¼ left (weight to left foot), touch R next to left (wall 6)

Sequence = 32 Steps
Step-Touch, Back Heel, K Step, Walk Around

Cupid Shuffle

Count: 32 **Wall:** 4 **Level:** Absolute Beginner
Choreographer: Unknown
Music: Cupid Shuffle - Cupid

Start: Vocals -- Weight on left foot (counter clockwise dance)

Section 1: Step Together to the Right Side, Step 4X
- 1-2 Step R foot to right, step L foot beside right foot
- 3-4 Step R foot to right, step L foot beside right foot
- 5-6 Step R foot side right, step L foot beside right foot
- 7-8 Step R foot side right, <u>touch</u> L foot beside right foot

Section 2: Step Together to Left Side (4X)
- 1-2 Step L foot side left, step R foot beside left foot
- 3-4 Step L foot side left, step R foot beside left foot
- 5-6 Step L foot side left, step R foot beside left foot
- 7-8 Step L foot side left <u>touch,</u> R foot beside left foot

Section 3: Heel Touches
- 1-2 Step R heel forward, step R foot next to left
- 3-4 Step L heel forward, step L foot next to right
- 5-6 Step R heel forward, step R foot next to left
- 7-8 Step L heel forward, <u>step</u> L foot next to right

Section 4: 1/4 Turning Left: 8 Count Begins on Right Foot
- 1-8 Step R foot turning ¼ to the left in 8 steps.. (RLRLRLRL)
  Take small steps. You will end up weight on left foot.

Rainy Night

Count: 32　**Wall:** 4　**Level:** Absolute Beginner
Choreographer: Pat Grillo - 2019
Music: I Love a Rainy Night, Eddie Rabbit

Start: Vocals -- Weight on left foot (clockwise dance)

Section 1: Toe Heel Struts 4X

1-2	Step forward on R toe, drop R heel
3-4	Step forward on L toe, drop L heel
5-6	Step forward on R toe, drop right heel
7-8	Step forward on L toe, drop left heel

Section 2: ¼ Right Turning K Step

1-2	Step R diagonally forward, touch L next to right
3-4	Step back to center, touch R next to left
5-6	Turn ¼ R, touch L next to R foot
7-8	Step L to L, touch R next to L

Section 3: R Grapevine with Touch; L Grapevine with Brush

1-3	Step R to right side, step L behind R, step R to right side
4	Touch L next to right foot
5-7	Step L to left side, step R behind left, step L to left side
8	Brush R next to left foot

Section 4: R Rocking Chair 2X

1-2	Rock forward on R, recover back on L foot
3-4	Rock backward on R, recover back on L foot
5-6	Rock forward on R, recover back on L foot
7-8	Rock backward on R, recover back on L foot

Electric Slide

Count: 18 **Wall:** 4 **Level:** Absolute Beginner
Choreographer: Ric Silver - 1976
Music: Electric Slide - Marcia Griffiths

Start: Vocals -- Weight on left foot (counter clockwise)

Section 1: Vine to the Right, Touch, Vine to the Left, Touch

- 1-2 Step R foot to right side, step L foot behind right foot
- 3-4 Step R to right side, touch L next to right foot
- 5-6 Step L foot to left side, step R foot behind left foot
- 7-8 Step L to left side, touch R next to left foot

Section 2: Walk 3 Steps Back RLR, Touch Left

- 1-3 Step R foot back, step L foot back, step R foot back
- 4 Touch L foot beside right foot

Rock Step L fwd, Touch R; Rock Step R Back, Touch L

- 5-6 Rock-step fwd on L foot, touch R foot next to L foot
- 7-8 Rock-step backward on R, touch L foot next to R

Section 3: Step, Turn with a Scuff

- 1-2 Turn 1/4 left on left foot, scuff R foot as you turn

Eye Candy EZ

Count: 32 **Wall:** 1   **Level:** Absolute Beginner
Choreographer: Pat Grillo - 2019
Music: Candyman: Christina Aguilera Eye Candy: Josh Turner Elvis Blessed My Soul

Start: Vocals -- Weight on left foot

Section 1: R & L Toe Struts; Touch R Out-in, Step L Out, Step R Next to R
- 1-2   Touch R toe forward, drop R heel
- 3-4   Touch L toe forward, drop L heel
- 5-6   Touch R toe to right side, touch R toe back next to left foot
- 7-8   Step R toe to right side, step L toe next to right foot

Section 2: L&R Toe Strut; Step L Out-in, Step L Out, Touch R Next to L
- 1-2   Touch L toe forward, drop L heel
- 3-4   Touch R toe forward, drop R heel
- 5-6   Touch L toe to left side, touch L toe next to right foot
- 7-8   Step L toe to left side, touch R toe next to left foot

Section 3: Step, Heel Touches
- 1-2   Step R foot back, touch L heel in place
- 2-4   Step L foot back, touch R heel in place
- 5-6   Step R foot back, touch L heel in place
- 7-8   Step L foot back, touch R heel in place

Section 4: Step Together, Step, Touch (R&L)
- 1-2   Step R foot to side, step L foot next to right foot
- 3-4   Step R foot to side, touch L foot next to right foot
- 5-6   Step L foot to side, step R foot next to left foot
- 7-8   Step L foot to left side, touch R foot next to left foot

I Fell in Love EZ

Count: 32 **Wall:** 1 **Level:** Absolute Beginner
Choreographer: Pat Grillo – August 2022
Music: I slipped and Fell in Love, Alan Jackson
I Like It, I Love It- Tim McGraw

Start: Vocals -- Weight on left foot

Section 1: Heel Struts Forward 4X
- 1-2 Step R heel forward, drop R toe
- 3-4 Step L heel forward, drop L toe
- 5-6 Step R heel forward, drop R toe
- 7-8 Step L heel forward, drop L toe

Section: 2: Walk Back 3 X RLR, Touch L, Stomp in place LRL 3 X, Touch R
- 1-2 Step R foot back, step L foot back
- 3-4 Step R foot back, touch L foot beside right foot
- 5-6 Stomp L foot in place, stomp R foot in place
- 7-8 Stomp L in place, touch R beside left foot

Section 3: R Grapevine, Touch L; L Grapevine, Touch R
- 1-2 Step R foot to right side, cross L foot behind right foot
- 3-4 Step right foot to right side, touch L foot beside right foot
- 5-6 Step L foot to left side, cross R foot behind left foot
- 7-8 Step L foot to left side, touch R foot beside left foot

Section 4 : Touch R Heel fwd, Step R Back; Repeat on Left, Jazz Box
- 1-2 Step R heel fwd, step R foot back
- 3-4 Step L heel fwd, step L foot back
- 5-6 Cross R foot over left, step left foot back
- 7-8 Step R foot to right side, step L foot next to right foot

Blackpool By the Sea EZ

Count: 32 **Wall:** 1 **Level:** Absolute Beginner
Choreographer: Pat Grillo – August 2017
Music: Blackpool By the Sea, David Sheriff

Start: Vocals -- Weight on left foot

Section 1: Charleston Step 2X

- 1-2 Swing R foot fwd, swing, R foot backward
- 3-4 Swing L foot backward, Swing L foot forward
- 5-6 Swing R foot fwd, swing R foot backward
- 7-8 Swing L foot backward, touch L foot forward

Section 2: Charleston Kicks 2X

- 1-2 Step R foot fwd, Kick L foot forward
- 3-4 Step L foot backward, touch R foot backward
- 5-6 Step R foot forward, kick L foot forward
- 7-8 Step L foot backward, touch R next to left foot

Section 3: R & LStep Back, Touch Heel with Salute 2X

- 1-2 Step R back, touch L heel diagonal forward
  Salute left hand to the head and right hand on the waist
- 3-4 Step L foot back, touch R heel diagonal forward
  Salute right hand to the head and left hand on the waist
- 5-8 Step R foot to R side, touch L next to right
- 7-8 Step L foot to L side, touch R next to L

Section 4: Step Together, Step Touch; 2X

- 1-2 Step R foot to R side, step L foot next to R foot
- 3-4 Step R foot to R side, touch L foot next to R foot
- 5-6 Step L foot to L side, step R foot next to L foot
- 7-8 Step L foot to L side, touch R foot next to L foot

Funky Town EZ

Count: 32   **Wall:** 4   **Level:** Absolute Beginner
Choreographer: Pat Grillo-2019
Music: Funky Town, Lipps Inc.

Section 1: K Step (clockwise)
- 1-2   Step R foot diagonally fwd, touch L foot next to R foot
- 3-4   Step L foot back to center, touch R foot next to L foot
- 5-6   Step R foot diagonally back, touch L foot next to R foot
- 7-8   Step L foot back to center, touch R foot next to L foot

Section 2: R Grapevine, Touch; L Grapevine, Touch
- 1-3   Step R foot to R side, step L foot behind R, step R foot to R side
- 4   Touch L foot next to right foot
- 5-7   Step L foot to L side, step R foot behind L foot, step L foot to L side
- 8   Touch R foot next to light foot

Section 3: V Step, Rocking Chair
- 1-2   Step R foot slightly fwd out to the right; step L foot slightly out to the L
- 3-4   Bring R foot back to center; bring L foot back to center
- 5-6   Rock R foot fwd, rock back on left foot
- 7-8   Rock R foot backward, rock L foot forward

Section 4: Rock to R Side, Recover, Stomp R, Scuff R; Jazz Box ¼ R Turn
- 1-2   Rock R, foot to right side; recover back on left foot
- 3-4   <u>Stomp</u> R foot; scuff right
- 5-6   Cross R foot over left foot, step L foot back,
- 7-8   ¼ right turn with weight ending on right, touch L foot next to right foot

Ten Tonne Truck EZ

Count: 32 **Wall:** 4 **Level:** Beginner
Choreographer: Pat Grillo - 2020
Music: Ten Tonne Truck - Tami Neilson

Start: Vocals -- Weight on left foot (counrter clockwise)

Section 1: Point Out-In x2 (RL)

- 1-2 Point R foot out to right side, touch R foot in next to L foot
- 3-4 Step R foot out to right side, step L foot next to R foot
- 5-6 Point L foot out to left side, touch L foot in next to R foot
- 7-8 Step L foot out to left side touch R foot next to L foot

Section 2: Rocking Chair, Stomp, Heel Bounces 3x, ¼ L Turn

- 1-2 Rock R foot forward, recover on L foot
- 3-4 Rock R foot backward, recover onto L foot
- 5 Stomp R foot forward; keeping feet apart
- 6-8 Bounce both heels 3 times making 1/4 turn left

Section 3: Step Diagonal Fwd, Step Together, Step Fwd, touch (R&L)

- 1-4 Step R foot diagonal fwd, step L foot next to R foot
- 3-4 Step R diagonal fwd, touch L foot next to R
- 5-6 Step L diagonal fwd, step R foot next to L,
- 7-8 Step L diagonal, touch R foot next to R

Section 4: Step Right Backward, Touch Left Heel in Place (4x)

- 1-2 Step R backward, touch L heel in place
- 3-4 Step L backward, touch R heel in place
- 5-6 Step R backward, touch L heel in place
- 7-8 Step L backward, touch R 0foot in place

Cowboy For a Night

Count: 32 **Wall:** 4 **Level:** Absolute Beginner
Choreographer: Pat Newell – 17th August 2018
Music: Cowboy For a Night - Australia's Tornadoes

Start: Vocals -- Weight on left foot (counter clockwise)

Section 1: Step Diagonal Together, Step Touch R&L

1-2	Step diagonal forward on R, step L next to R
3-4	Step diagonal forward on R, touch L next to R
5-6	Step diagonal forward on L, step R next to L
7-8	Step diagonal forward on L, touch R next to L

Section2 Steps & Touches going back slightly Zig Zag pattern (4X)

1-2	Step back on R, touch L
3-4	Step back on L touch R
5-6	Step back on R, touch L
7-8	Step back on L touch R

Section 3: RIght Vine with Touch, Left Vine ¼ Turn with Brush

1-3	Step R to R, L behind R, step R to right
4	Touch L beside R
5-6	Step L to L, R behind L
7-8	Step L with ¼ L turn, brush R fwd (9:00)

Right Rocking Chair 2X

1-2	Rock fwd on R, recover on L
3-4	Rock back on R, recover on L
5-6	Rock fwd on R, recover on L
7-8	Rock back on R, recover on L

Be Bop EZ

Count: 32 **Wall:** 4 **Level:** Absolute Beginner
Choreographer: Larry Bass - January 2019
Music: Be Bop A Lula by Scooter Lee

Start: Vocals -- Weight on left foot (clockwise)

Section1: K Step
- 1-2 Step R diagonal fwd to right, touch L beside foot
- 3-4 Step L back to center, touch R foot beside left foot
- 5-6 Step R diagonal back to right, touch left foot beside right foot
- 7-8 Step L forward back to center, touch right foot beside left foot

Section 2: 3 Walks forward, Kick; 3 walks back, touch
- 1-4 Walk forward R, L R foot, kick L foot forward
- 5-8 Walk back L, R, L foot, touch R foot beside L foot

Section 3: Cross, Point (R&L), Behind, Point 2X
- 1-2 Step R foot across L foot, point L foot to left
- 3-4 Step L foot across R; Point R foot to right foot
- 5-6 Step R foot behind L foot, point L foot to left
- 7-8 Step L behind R foot, point R foot slightly forward

Section 4: Jazz Box, Jazz Box With ¼ Turn
- 1-2 Step R foot across L foot, step L back
- 3-4 Step R next to L foot, step L foot next to R foot
- 5-6 Step R foot across L foot, step L foot back
- 7-8 Turn R ¼, step L foot next to right foot

Livin' On Love EZ

Count: 32   **Wall:** 2   **Level:** Absolute Beginner
Choreographer: Pat Grillo-2021
Music: Livin' On Love by Alan Jackson

Start: Vocals -- Weight on left foot (counter clock wise

Section 1: Vine Right, Scuff; Left Rocking Chair
- 1-3   Step R to right side, step L foot behind right foot, step R foot to right
- 4   Scuff L foot fwd
- 5-6   Rock fwd on L foot, recover on right foot
- 7-8   Rock back on L foot, recover on right foot

Section 2: Vine Left/ Scuff, Rocking Chair
- 1-3   Step L to left side, R behind left foot, step L foot to left
- 4   Scuff R foot fwd
- 5-6   Rock fwd on R, recover on left foot
- 7-8   Rock back on R foot, recover on left foot

Section 3: R&L Heel Locks with Brush
- 1-2   Step fwd on R foot, lock L foot behind right foot
- 3-4   Step fwd on R foot, brush L foot fwd
- 5-6   Step fwd on L foot, lock R foot behind L foot
- 7-8   Step fwd on L, brush R foot fwd

Section 4: Step Touch, Walk Around
- 1-2   Step fwd R foot, touch L foot next to right foot
- 3-4   Turn ¼ left on L foot, touch R foot next to left foot
- 5-6   Step R foot to right side, touch L foot next to right foot
- 7-8   Turn ¼ L on left foot, touch R next to left foot

Sure You Are

Count: 32 **Wall:** 1 **Level:** Absolute Beginner
Choreographer: Larry Bass
Music: But I Am A Good Girl by Christina Aguilera

Start: Vocals -- Weight on left foot

Section 1: R&L Fwd Step-Cross Kicks, 3 Walk, Fwd Kick
- 1-2 Step R foot forward, kick L foot across right foot
- 3-4 Step L foot forward; kick R foot across left foot
- 5-7 Walk fwd right, left, right foot (R L R)
- 8   Kick L foot forward

Section 2: R&L Backward Step Cross-Kicks; 2 Walk Back, Touch
- 1-2 Step L foot back, kick R foot across left foot
- 3-4 Step R foot back, kick L across right foot
- 5-6 Walk L foot back, walk R foot back
- 7-8 Step L foot to left, touch R foot next to left foot

Section 3: R&L Step-Cross Kicks, R Vine, Kick
- 1-2 Step R foot to right side, kick L foot across right foot
- 3-4 step L foot to left side, kick R foot across left foot
- 5-6 Step R foot to right side, step L foot behind R
- 7-8 Step R to right side, kick L foot across R foot

Section 4: L Vine, Kick, Jazz Square
- 1-2 Step L foot to left side, cross R behind left foot
- 3-4 Step L foot to left side, kick R foot over left foot
- 5-6 Cross R foot over L foot, step L foot back
- 7-8 Step R to right side, step L foot next to right foot

Chocolate Melon

Count: 32 **Wall:** 4 **Level:** Beginner
Choreographer: Larry Bass
Music: Coco Melon - Jessica Jay

Start: Vocals -- Weight on left foot (counter clockwise)

Section 1: R -V Step, R Diagonal fwd, R Step-Slide, R Step-Brush
- 1-2   Step R diagonally right, step L foot diagonal left
- 3-4   Step R back to center; step L back to center
- 5-6   Step R foot fwd diagonal, slide L next to right
- 7-8   Step R to right diagonal, brush L beside right

Section 2: L-V Step; L Diagonal fwd, L Step-Slide, L Step-Brush
- 1-2   Step L to left diagonal, step R to right diagonal
- 3-4   Step L back to center; step R back to center
- 5-6   Step L to left diagonal; Slide R next to left
- 7-8   Step L to left diagonal, brush R beside left

Section 3: Cross-Rock-Recover, R Step, L Cross, R Vine with cross.
- 1-2   Rock R across L, recover back to L
- 3-4   Step R to right, step L across R foot
- 5-6   Step R to right, step L behind right
- 7-8   Step R to right, step L across right

Section 4: Turn 1/4 Left with 1/8 Hip Rolls , Hip Roll Turn; Jazz Square
- 1-2,   Turning 1/8 to left, step R forward, roll hips counter clockwise
- 3-4   Step R forward, roll hips counter clockwise turning 1/8 turn left
- 5-6   Step R across L, step L back;
- 7-8   Step R to right, step L next to right

Country Line

Count: 32 **Wall:** 4 **Level:** Beginner
Choreographer: Pat Grillo 2017
Music: Gonna Come Back as a Country Song by Alan Jackson

Start: Vocals -- Weight on left foot (clockwise)

Section 1: K Step
- 1-2   Step R diagonally fwd, touch L next to right foot
- 3-4   Step L back to center, touch R next to L foot
- 5-6   Step R diagonally backward, touch L foot next to L foot
- 7-8   Step L diagonally forward, touch R foot next to L

Section 2: R Vine with Brush, L Vine with Brush
- 1-2   Step R foot to right side, cross L foot behind right foot
- 3-4   Step right to right side, brush L forward
- 5-6   Step L foot to left side, cross R foot behind right foot
- 7-8   Step L to left side, brush R forward

Section 3: R Lock Step fwd with Brush. L Lock Step with Brush
- 1-2   Step R foot diagonally forward, lock L foot behind right,
- 3-4   Step R foot fwd, brush left foot forward
- 5-6   Step L foot diagonally forward, lock R foot behind right,
- 7-8   Step L foot fwd, brush R foot forward

Section 4: Jazz Box, Jazz Box with 1/4 Turn
- 1-2   Cross R foot over left, step L foot back
- 3-4   Step R next to right side, step L foot next to right foot
- 5-6   Cross R foot over left, step L foot back
- 7-8   Turn R to right side, step L foot next to right

Come Dance with Me

Count: 32 **Wall:** 4 **Level:** Beginner
Choreographer: Jo Thompson Szymanski
Music: Come Dance with Me - Nancy Hays
Some Gave All- Billy Ray Cyrus

Start: Vocals -- Weight on left foot (counter clockwise)

Section 1 R Lock Step, Brush L Lock Step Brush
- 1-3 Step R diagonally fwd, lock L behind R foot, step R diagonally fwd
- 4 Brush left forward
- 5-7 Step L diagonally fwd, lock R behind L, step L diagonally forward
- 8 Brush R forward

Section 2 Jazz Box wiith Cross, Weave
- 1-4 Cross R over L, step L back, step R to side, cross L over R
- 5-6 Step R to side, cross L behind R
- 7-8 Step R to side, cross L over R

Section 3 R Scissors, Hold: L Scissors, Hold
- 1-3 Step R to side, step L together, cross R over L
- 4 Hold
- 5-7 Step L to side, step R together, cross L over right
- 8 Hold

Section 4 R Scissors, Step L, Cross R behind L, Turn 1/4 L, Pivot 1/2 L
- 1-3 Step R to side, step L together, cross R over L
- 4 Step L to L side
- 5-6 Cross R behind L. turn 1/4 L {weight is on left foot)
- 7-8 Step R foot fwd, L pivot 1/2 turn left

Shotgun Jenny

Count: 32 **Wall:** 32 **Level:** Beginner
Choreographer: Kathy Brown (USA) - May 2012
Music: Shake it (feat. Big & Rich) - The Lacs

Start: Vocals -- Weight on left foot (counter clockwise)

Section 1: Right Heel, Left Heel, 2x Right Kick, Rock, Recover
- 1-2   Tap R heel forward, step R next to left foot
- 3-4   Tap L heel forward, step L next to left foot
- 5-6   Kick R fwd, kick R fwd
- 7-8   Rock back on R foot, recover on L foot

Section 2: Step R, Touch L, Step L, Touch R, Vine R, L Scuff
- 1-2   Step R to right side, touch L foot next to right foot
- 3-4   Step L to side, touch R foot next to left foot
- 5-6   Step R to side, step L behind right foot
- 7-8   Step R to right side, scuff L foot

Section 3: Vine L with 1/4 Turn L, Scuff R, 3 Right Hip Bumps, Brush
- 1-2   Step L to side, step R behind left foot
- 3-4   Step L with a 1/4 turn to L, scuff R foot
- 5-6   Step down on R, push R hip forward, push R hip back
- 7-8   Push R hip forward, brush L foot forward

Section 4: Step L Down, 3 L Hip Bumps, Brush, Turn 1/4 L with 2 Hip Rolls
- 1-2,   Step L down. push L hip forward, push L hip back
- 3-4   Push L hip forward, brush R foot
- 5-6   Step R foot fwd, roll hips while turning 1/8 L
- 7-8   Continue turning 1/8 L with hip rolls

Introduction to Syncopation

Now that you are aware of the difference between steps, touches and weight change, it's time to move on to syncopated steps.

Syncopated steps have an extra step between beats and is marked by an ampersand. So if a step sheet is marked or a leader calls 1 and 2, she/he is saying *squeeze a half-beat between two musical beats*.

You know you're a dancer when "AND" is a number

& means syncopated beat count

1 & 2
slow fast slow

— means one step per beat

1 - 2
beat beat

Two Step

Count: 16 **Wall:** 4 **Level:** Beginner
Choreographer: Robert Royston (USA) - May 2013
Music: Two Step (Feat. Colt Ford) - Laura Bell Bundy

Start: Vocals -- Weight on left foot (counter clockwise)

Section 1: Step R, Step L Beside Right ; Sync R Triple Step
- 1-2 Step R foot to right side, step L foot next to right side
- 3&4 Step R foot to R side (&) step L foot next to right; step R to left (RLR)
- 5-6 Step L foot to left side, step R foot next to right side
- 7&8 Step L foot to L side (&) step R foot next to L, step L foot to left (LRL)

Section 2: R Kick-Ball-Change 2X; 4 Skates Turning L RLRL
- 1&2 Kick R foot fwd, return R foot back to center, change weight to L foot
- 3&4 Kick R foot fwd, return R foot back to center, change weight to L foot
- 5-8 Skate R, L, R, turn ¼ to the L weight ending on the L

Listen to the music. Be prepared for a change in the music.in the 8th sequence (9 o'clock wall) and the 9th sequence in (12 o"clock wall).

EZ Shuffle

Count: 32 **Wall:** 4 **Level:** Beginner
Choreographer: Larry Bass
Music: Cowboy Up by Amy Clawson

Start: Vocals -- Weight on left foot (clockwise)

Section 1: R Toe In, R Heel In, Heel, Triple Step R&L
- 1-2 Touch R toe in, touch R heel in
- 3&4 Step R foot (&) step left foot; step R foot in place (RLR)
- 5-6 Touch L toe in, touch L heel in
- 7&8 Step left foot (&) step on right foot; step left foot in place (LRL)

Section 2: Charleston Kicks
- 1-2 Step right foot forward, kick left foot out
- 3-4 Step left foot back, touch right foot back
- 5-6 Step right forward, kick left foot out
- 7-8 Step left back, touch right foot back

Section 3 : Diagonal Shuffles Forward 4x
- 1&2 Step fwd on R foot (&) step L foot next to right, step R foot fwd
- 3&4 Step fwd on L foot (&) step R foot next to left foot, step L fwd.
- 5&6 Step fwd on R foot (&) step L foot next to right foot, step R fwd
- 7&8 Step fwd on L foot (&) step R foot next to left foot, step L fwd.

Section 4: Jazz Square; Jazz square with ¼ Turn
- 1-2 Step R foot across L foot; step L foot back
- 3-4 Step R foot to right side; step L foot beside right foot
- 5-6 Step R foot across left foot; step L foot back
- 7-8 Turn ¼ stepping R foot to right side; step L beside right foot

Honey I'm Good

Count: 32 **Wall:** 4 **Level:** Beginner
Choreographer: Suza Beau -2015
Music: Honey I'm Good - Andy Grammar

Start: Vocals -- Weight on left foot (counter clockwise)

Section 1: R&L Toe In, Heel In, Triple Step
- 1-2 Touch R toes in next to left foot, touch R heel in next to left foot
- 3&4 Step in place R foot (&) step L foot; step R foot (RLR)
- 5-6 Touch L toes in next to right, touch L heel in next to right foot
- 7&8 Step in place L foot (&) step R foot; step L foot (LRL)

Section 2: V Step; Step Touch (R&L)
- 1-2 Step R foot out diagonally forward, step L foot diagonally out
- 3-4 Step R foot back in, step L foot next to right
- 5-6 Step R foot to right side, touch L foot next to right
- 7-8 Step L to left side, touch R next to left foot

Section 3: Side Cross, Side Kick, Side Cross, Side Kick
- 1-2 Step R to right side, cross L foot over right
- 3-4 Step R to right side, kick L foot to left diagonal
- 5-6 Step left to left side, cross right over left
- 7-8 Step left to left side, kick right to right diagonal

Section 4: Rock Back Recover, Step Pivot 1/4, Jazz box
- 1-2 Rock back on right, recover on left foot
- 3-4 Step forward on R, pivot 1/4 left (weight on left)
- 5-6 Cross R foot over L foot, step L foot back
- 7-8 Step R to right side, step L foot next to right foot

Live Laugh Line Dance

Count: 32 **Wall:** 4 **Level:** Absolute Beginner
Choreographer: Pat Grillo - 2021
Music: Live Laugh Line Dance - Pauline Brown
Completely - Caro Emerald

Start: Vocals -- Weight on left foot (counter clockwise)

Section 1: (R&L) Cross, Point, (R&L) Behind, Point
1-2 Cross R foot over left foot, point L toe out
3-4 Cross L foot over right foot, point R toe out
5-6 Cross R foot behind L foot, point L toe out
7-8 Cross L foot behind right foot, point R toe out
  Stretch arms up when pointing

Section 2: (3X) Step-Heel Touches, 1/2 ShuffleTurn Left
1-2 Step back on R foot, touch L heel
3-4 Step L foot to left side, touch R heel next to left foot
5-6 Step R foot to right side, touch L foot next to right foot
7&8 Step L 1/4 turn to L, (&) touch R, step turn L
  Bend knees when touching heels down

Section 3: Jazz Box, Jazz Box with 1/4 R Turn
1-2 Cross R foot over left foot, step back on L foot
3-4 Step R next to left foot, step L next to right foot
5-6 Cross right over left, step left back
7-8 Turn 1/4 right on R, touch left next to right

Section 4: V Step, Rocking Chair
1-2 Step R foot diagonal fwd, step L foot diagonal fwd
2-3 Step R foot back to center, step L foot back to center
5-6 Rock R foot fwd, recover back on L foot
7-8 Rock R foot backward, recover on left foot

River Bank EZ

Count: 32 **Wall:** 1 **Level:** Beginner
Choreographer: Pat Grillo - 2020
Music: Riverbank- Whosoever
Cool Cat in Town - Tape Five

Start: Vocals -- Weight on left foot

Section 1 Charleston Step 2X
- 1-2 Swing R foot fwd, touch R foot backward
- 3-4 Swing L foot backward, touch L foot forward
- 5-6 Swing R foot fwd, swing R foot backward
- 7-8 Swing L foot backward, swing L foot forward

Section 2 Charleston Kicks 2X
- 1-2 Step R foot forward, kick L foot forward
- 3-4 Step L foot backward, touch R foot backward
- 5-6 Step R foot forward, kick L foot forward
- 7-8 Step L foot backward, touch R foot backward

Section 3: Touch R Fwd, Touch R to Side, Triple Step R &L
- 1 Touch R foot fwd (push hands down in front)
- 2 Touch R foot right side (push hands to sides)
- 3&4 Step R next to left foot (&) step L in place, Step R next to right
- 5 Touch L foot fwd (push hands down in front)
- 6 Touch L foot left side (push hands to sides)
- 7&8 Step L next to & step R in place, step L next to right goot

Section 4: Kick Ball Change 2X; Sailor Step R & L
- 1&2 Kick right foot forward (&) recover on the ball of right foot. step left in place.
- 3&4 Kick right foot forward (&) recover on the ball of right foot. step left in place
- 5&6 Step R foot behind L (&) step L beside R, step R foot forward.
- 7&8 Step L foot behind R (&) step R beside L, step L foot forward.

Monkey Around

Count: 32 **Wall:** 4 **Level:** Beginner
Choreographer: Doris O'Bryant Wilkie July 2016
Music: Monkey Around - Travis Trill

Start: Vocals -- Weight on left foot (counter clockwise)

Section1 Sailor Step R&L, Kick Ball Change 2X
1&2 Step R foot behind L (&) step L foot beside R; step the R foot fwd
3&4 Step L foot behind R (&) step R foot beside R; step the L foot fwd
5&6 Kick right foot forward (&) recover on ball of right foot, step left in place
7&8 Kick right foot forward (&) recover on ball of right foot. step left in place

Section 2 Fwd Rock/Recover, Triple ½ Turn, Fwd Rock, Triple ¼ Left Turn
1-2 Rock forward R foot, recover on L foot
3&4 ½ triple turn (6 oclock) (RLR)
5-6 Rock forward on L foot, recover on R foot
7&8 ¼ turn (9 oclock wall (LRL)

Section 3   R Cross Point, L Cross Point, Jazz Box
1-2 Cross R foot over L foot, point L foot to left side
3-4 Cross L foot over right foot, point R foot to right side
5-6 Cross R food over L, step L foot back
7-8   Step L foot next to right side, touch L foot next to right foot

Section 4 Rocking Chair, Jump R Fwd, Jump L Back
1-2 Rock R foot forward, recover on Lfoot
3-4 Rock back on R foot, recover on L foot
5-6 Jump R foot forward, jump L foot next to right foot
7-8 Jump R foot back, jump L foot back next to right foot

Jack I'm Mellow

Count: 32 **Wall:** 4 **Level:** Beginner
Choreographer: Roger Neff
Music: Jack I'm Mellow by Asleep at the Wheel

Start: Vocals -- Weight on left foot (clockwise)

Section 1: Charleston, Touch, Touch & Back, Left Coaster Step
- 1-2   Swing & touch R toe forward, step R foot backward
- 3-4   Swing & touch L toe back, step L forward
- 5-6   Touch R toe forward, step R foot backward
- 7&8   Step back on L foot, step back on R, step forward on L

Section 2: R&L Lock ; Jazz Box with ¼ Turn R with L to R
- 1&2   Step R foot forward, lock L behind R foot, step forward on R (RLR)
- 3&4   Step forward on L foot, lock R behind L, step forward on L (LRL)
- 5-6   Cross R foot over L foot, step L foot back
- 7-8   Turn R foot ¼ to R, cross L foot over R

Section 3: R & L Mamo, Rumba Box
- 1&2   Rock to R, recover on L, step R beside L,
- 3&4   Rock to L, recover on R, step L beside R
- 5&6   Step to R, step L beside R, step forward on R
- 7&8   Step to L, step R beside L, step back on L

Section 4: Step Back R L. Coaster Step, Walk Fwd L R, Lock Steps
- 1-2,   Step back on R, step back on L
- 3&4   Step R back, step L beside R, step fwd on R (RLR)
- 5-6   Walk forward L, R,
- 7&8   Step fwd on L, lock R behind L foot, step fwd on L (LRL)

Broken & Beautiful

Count: 32 **Wall:** 1 **Level:** Beginner
Choreographer - Lynne Herman & David Herman
Music: Let's Walk - Austin De Lone

Start: Vocals -- Weight on left foot (counter clockwise)

Section 1: Walk x2, Shuffle-fwd, Fwd-rock, Recover, Coaster-Cross
- 1-2   Step R foot fwd, step L foot forward
- 3&4   Step R fwd, (&) step L beside, step R fwd
- 5-6   Rock L forward, recover weight to R foot
- 7&8   Step L back, (&) step R beside L, cross L foot in front of R foot

Section 2: R Side, Together, Shuffle-fwd, L Fwd-rock, recover, ¼ Shuffle Turn
- 1-2   Step R to right side, step L foot beside R foot
- 3-4   Step R foot fwd,(&) step L foot beside R foot step R fwd
- 5-6   Rock L foot forward, recover weight to R foot
- 7&8   Step L foot to left side,turn R (&),step R beside L,step L fwd

Section 3: Cross-point R, Cross Point L; Jazz-Box
- 1-2   Step R across L, point L foot to left side
- 3-4   Step L across R, point R foot to right side
- 5-6   Step R foot across, L foot, step L foot backward
- 7-8   Step R foot across, L foot, step L foot backward

Section 4: V Step, 2X R Kick-Ball-Change
- 1-2,   Step R foot forward slightly out, step L forward slightly out
- 3-4   Step R foot back to center, step L foot back to center
- 5&6   Kick R fwd, (&) quickly replace R beside left, shift weight to L foot
- 7-8   Kick R fwd, (&) quickly replace R beside left, shift weight to L foot

Chilly Cha Cha

Count: 32 **Wall:** 1 **Level:** Beginner
Choreographer - LaVon W Duke
Music: Chilly Cha Cha - Jessica Jay

Start: Vocals -- Weight on right foot (clockwise)

Section 1: L&R Cross Rock/Recover, Cha Cha Cha

1-2 Cross L foot over right foot, recover on right foot
3&4 Step L foot left (&) step R next to left, step L foot left: Add rhythm (LRL)
5-6 Cross right foot over left, recover on left foot
7&8 Step R foot right (&) step L foot next to right step R right (Add rhythm (RLR)

Section 2: Weave right, Cross Rock, Recover, Cha Cha Cha

1-4 Cross L over R, step R to right, cross L behind R, step R to right side
5-6 Cross L over R , recover on R
7&8 Cha cha cha (LRL)

Section 3 Weave Left, Cross Rock Recover, Cha Cha Cha

1-4 Cross R over L, step L to L side, cross R behind L, step L to left
5-6 Cross R over L, recover L
7&8 Cha cha cha right-left-right (RLR)

Section 4: Pivot ½ Turn R, Cha Cha Cha, Pivot ½ TurnL, Cha Cha Cha

1-2 Step L foot fwd ½ turn to right (facing 6:00)
3&4 Cha cha cha (LRL)
5-6 Step right foot fwd, ½ turn to left (facing 12:00)
7&8 Cha Cha Cha right (RLR)

High Class

Count: 32 **Wall:** 4 **Level:** Beginner
Choreographer: Frédéric Marchand (FR) - May 2020
Music: High Class White Trash - Jeremy Egg Band

Start: Vocals -- Weight on right foot (clockwise)

Section 1: Rocking Chair, Triple Step R, Fwd, Rock L Back, Recover

1-4   Step R foot fwd, recover on left foot, step R foot back, recover on left
5&6   Step R foot to right side (&) L foot together, step R foot to right side
7-8   Step left back, recover on right foot

Section 2: Weave Left, Side Triple Left, Rock Step Back Right, Recover

1-4   Step L to left side, cross R behind left, step L to left, cross R over lefl
5&6   Step L to left side, (&) together, step L to left side
7-8   Step R foot back, recover on L foot

Section 3: 1/4 R Monterey , 1/4 Heel Grind turn R, Step back R, Hook Left

1-2   Point R foot out, make 1/4 R turn bringing R foot in as you turn
3-4   Point L foort out, bring left next to R (weight ends on left)
5-6   Step R heel fwd, make 1/4 grind to the right, recover on L (weight ends on L (6 o"clock)
7-8   Step R back, hook L cross over R

Section 4: L Lock Step with Brush, Pivot 1/2 Turn L, Pivot 1/4 Turn L

1-3   Step left fwd, lock R behind left, step L fwd,
4   Brush R foot
5-6   Step R fwd,1/2 turn L (weight on Left) (12 o'clock)

Now, find yourself a dance group; your body and mind will love you!

You have learned 27 dances and 37 line dance steps

Bounce	Jazz Box	Scissors
Brush	Jump	Scuff
Cha Cha	K Step	Shuffle
Charleston Kick	Kick	Side Cross
Coatser Step	Kick Ball Change	Stomp
Charlestons Step	Lock Step	Toe Strut
Cross Point	Mambo	Triple Step
Grapevine	Montery Turn	Turn
Fan	Pivot	V Step
Heel Grind	Rock/Recover	Walk Around
Heel Touch	Rocking Chair	Weave
Heel Sturt	Mambo	
Hitch	Sailer Step	

How to Read A Step Sheet
&
Step Glossary

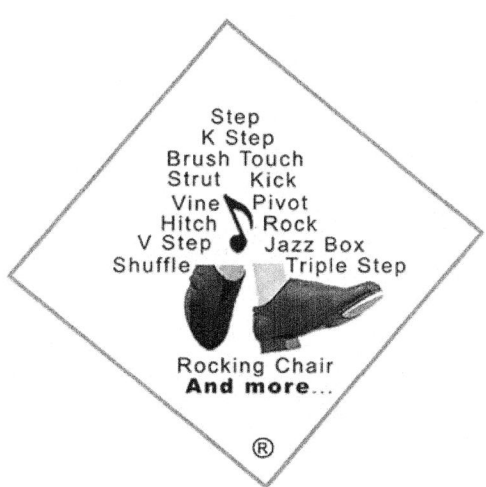

How To Read A Step Sheet

Step sheets are written by the dance choreographer and consist of all the necessary information needed to perform the dance.

1. .Name of Dance

2. Dancing information such as: Step count, number of walls, level of dance, choreographer, music and artist.

3. This is the **signal** to begin dancing. Generally, a dance starts on the lyrics, but not always. Some time it will begin on a specific beat count such as 16, 24 or 32 beats. It depends on how the introduction to the song was introduced. It is important to start at the precise time in order to be *on beat.*

4. Dances are organized in **4 sections of 8 steps.** The first line in each section is called the heading and contains the proper name of the steps in that section

5. **Step numbers & symbols:** Steps that are numbered with a hyphen **(1-2)** signals the dancer that each step counts as one beat. Steps numbers with a ampersand **(1&2)** signals that the steps are syncopated (extra step added between beats).

6. **Instructions:** Breaks down the dance step-by-step; clarifies how to execute each step and the direction to turn (½ right turn).

EZ Shuffle

Count: 32 **Wall:** 4 **Level:** Beginner
Choreographer: Larry Bass
Music: Cowboy Up by Amy Clawson

Start: Vocals -- Weight on left foot

Section 1: R Toe-Heel, Triple Step R&L
- 1-2   Touch right toe beside L foot, touch right heel beside L foot
- 3&4   Step right foot (&) step left foot; step right foot in place (RLR)
- 5-6   Touch left toe beside R foot, touch left heel beside R foot
- 7&8   Step left foot (&) step on right foot; step left foot in place (LRL)

Section 2: Charleston Kicks
- 1-2   Step right foot forward, kick left foot out
- 3-4   Step left foot back, touch right foot back
- 5-6   Step right forward, kick left foot out
- 7-8   Step left back, touch right foot back

Section 3 : Diagonal Shuffles Forward 4x
- 1&2   Step fwd on right foot (&) step left foot next to right, step right foot fwd
- 3&4   Step fwd on left foot (&) step right foot next to left foot, step left fwd.
- 5&6   Step fwd on right foot (&) step left foot next to right foot, step right fwd
- 7&8   Step fwd on left foot (&) step right foot next to left foot, step left fwd.

Section 4: Jazz Square; Jazz square with ¼ Turn
- 1-2   Step right foot across left; step left back
- 3-4   Step right foot to right side; step left foot beside right
- 5-6   Step right across left; step left back
- 7-8   Turn ¼ turn right stepping right foot to right side; step left beside right

Step Glossary

1 Count Steps

Brush	Push ball of foot forward and upwards past the weight bearing foot.
Drag	Drag one foot next to the other foot (Slide).
Freeze	Hold position for one count beat.
Flick	Brush foot forward and upwards past the weight bearing foot with the heel make contact with the floor.
Bump	Bump hips to the right, left, backwards or forwards with beat to the music.
Hip Roll	Move hips in a upward rolling motion.
Hitch	Lift knee.
Hold	Freeze your position for a one count beat.
Paddle	Foot stationary on the floor. turn with boat paddle motion
Recover	Return to previous foot.
Scuff	Push the foot forward and upwards, past the weight bearing foot with the heel making contact with the floor.
Touch	Touch toe to floor without transferring weight. It is a signal to make the next step using the same foot.
Step	Transfer weight by transferring to other foot.
Slide	Slide one foot next to the other foot. (Drag)
Stomp	Stomp foot on the floor.
Walk	Shift shift weight from one foot to the other

2 Count Steps

Cross Step	Cross right foot over left foot; point left foot out to side
Fans	Keep right heel in contact with floor; move toes out to side and back in.

Heel Grind	Step R heel fwd, make 1/4 grind to the right, recover on L
Heel Strut	Step right foot heel forward on the floor with toes raised; drop toes to the floor and place weight on foot.
Heel Touch	Touch heel of foot forward
Pivot Turn	Foot stationary on the floor, step fwd on right foot and turn like clock dail. Pivots can be 1/4. 1/2, 3/4 or complete turn
Rock Step	Step right foot forward and rock; the stationary foot will lift slightly off the floor, shift weight back onto the stationary foot. *Rock forwards, backwards or sideways).*
Toe Struts	Step right foot forward on the floor with toes raised, drop the heel and place weight on foot. *(Strut forward or backward)*

3 Count Steps

Mambo Step next to L foot	Weight on left foot: Rock to the right, recover on L foot, step R foot
Rolling Turn	Facing front wall: ¼ turn with right foot facing right wall, ½ turn right stepping back on left, ¼ turn stepping right to right side. *Turn is followed by a left foot touch next to the right.*
R & L Vines	Step *right* to the side; step lerft foot behind the right foot; step right foot next to right side. *Vines are followed by a 1-count step.*

The steps below can be counted as 3 steps or as 2 snyncopated steps. Syncopated steps are signaled by an ampersand (&) whereas single counts are signaled by a hyphen (-).

Coaster Step	Step right foot back, step left foot back, step right foot forward or cross,
Lock Step	Step right foot forward, step left foot behind right foot, step right foot forward.
Rumba Step	Step to R, step L beside R, step R forward

4 Count Steps

Charleston Kicks Step right foot forward, kick left foot forward, step left foot back, touch right foot next to left.

Charleston Step Swing right foot forward, swing right foot back, swing left foot back, swing left foot forward.

Jazz Box	Step right foot across in front of left foot, step left foot back, step right foot to the right side, step left foot next to right foot.
Rumba Box	Step to R, Step L beside R, Step forward on R, Step to L, step R beside L, Step back on L
V Step	Step right foot diagonally to right, step left foot to left side (shoulder width apart), step right back center, step left foot next to right foot.
Weave	Step next to R L over R, step R to right, cross L behind R, step R to right

8 Count Step

K step	Step right foot diagonally fwd to right, touch left foot next to right, step left foot back to center, touch right foot next to left, step right foot diagonally back, touch left foot next to left, step left foot to center, touch right foot next to left

Syncopated Steps (&)

Cha Cha Cha	Step right foot (&) step left foot; Step right foot: Add rhythm.
Chassé	Step right foot to right side (&) step left foot next to right foot; step right foot to right side. (left or right side)
Heel Jacks	Step right heel forward (&) step right foot back; Cross left foot over right. *Repeat on left foot.*
Kick Ball	Kick right foot forward (&) recover on the ball of right foot. step left foot in place.
Coaster Step	Step right foot back (&) step left foot back next to right; Step forward on right foot.
Lock Step	Step right foot forward, (&) step left foot behind right foot, step right foot forward.
Sailor Step	Step right foot behind left (&) step left foot beside right; Step the R right footforward.
Shuffle	Step forward on right foot (&) step left foot next to right foot; step right foot forward. Traveling step
Triple Step	Step right foot (&) step left foot; step right foot or stepping in place

Instruction Videos

intro

rainy night

Blackpool by the sea_demo

live laugh march 26

Visit: StepsandBeats.com

Everything you need to know about line dancing

Visit StepsandBeats.com

"Add years to your life
and life to your years"

Instructor: Pat Grillo
https://www.youtube.com/@patgrillo3123

Contact Pat
Website: stepsandbeats.com
Email: patgrillo1@gmail.com
Facebook.com/linedancingwithpatgrillo

Printed in Great Britain
by Amazon